W9-ASK-689

MAKING SENSE

MAKING SENSE

Animal Perception and Communication

Bruce Brooks

Farrar Straus Giroux • *New York*

In association with Thirteen/WNET

Other books by Bruce Brooks in the KNOWING NATURE series

Nature by Design
Predator!

For Alexander and Spencer

*Published simultaneously in Canada by HarperCollins*Canada*Ltd*
Color separations by Hong Kong Scanner
Printed and bound in the United States of America
by Worzalla Publishing
FIRST EDITION, 1993

Library of Congress Cataloging-in-Publication Data
Brooks, Bruce.
Making sense : animal perception and communication / Bruce Brooks.—1st ed.
p. cm. — (Knowing nature)
Includes index.
*Summary: Discusses animals' six senses—seeing, hearing, smelling,
tasting, touching, and feeling—and how they use them to perceive
and react to the world around them.*
*1. Senses and sensation—Juvenile literature. 2. Perception in
animals—Juvenile literature. [1. Senses and sensation.
2. Animals.] I. Title. II. Series.*
QP431.B67 1993 591.1'82—dc20 93-10474 CIP AC

Contents

Knowing

One day while I was snorkeling around an island in the Caribbean Sea, I swam into a small bay and the clear, slightly turquoise water turned into mercury. Or at least that is how it seemed. One second I was slipping effortlessly through liquid crystal; the next second I was stuck inside a thick silver mass that pulsated on every side with the current. I felt I was about to smother, though I continued to breathe (or, to be honest, to gasp) perfectly well through my snorkel.

The sensation of being completely enclosed in some solid substance came largely from my sudden inability to see anything but pure silver: I had been used to seeing every little thing underwater brilliantly, but now the silver blocked out the bottom, the surface above me, and the busy coral reef that had been on both sides just a moment ago. What had happened? I forced myself to hang still in the water, breathing normally, trying to believe this was a weird illusion that would recede in a moment and leave me with an understanding. It took me a full half minute to figure out that I had swum into the midst of a huge school of small silver fish.

The fish were suspended in the water right up against me, like a mercury shirt. I focused on one, then the next, then the next, and saw that they held themselves apart by the smallest of margins, a few molecules of water winding between the scales and fins. The current was faint—a lilting in-and-out—but the mass of tiny fish made it oppressively visible as they moved with it in perfect unison. I pulled my head back, but my scalp touched nothing, and the fish in front of me still hung less than an inch from the glass of my diving mask. I swept my right arm upward in a slash, but not a fin did I touch, though there were fish surrounding every finger. I wiggled my fingers; the fish moved with the wiggles, always remaining the same short distance away.

After a while I made myself start swimming. It was the same eerie feeling of being encased in a solid mass, yet staying untouched and free-floating. No matter how sudden my movements were, the fish anticipated them and moved exactly the same distance in the same direction, as a unit.

I was just getting kind of comfortable with this odd communion when I felt something happen in the water. I wasn't at all sure how I perceived it—it wasn't a feeling that came from one sense over another—but I knew, in every part of my body, that something big was approaching. Something heavy. The fish around me seemed to thrum with alertness, and in that instant I was just one of them, waiting to see what came around the corner of the reef.

The tension in the water grew; my body, detached from my nice, cool intellect, got keen and rigid, ready to dart this way or that. The experience was fascinating: one part of me was amazed at the way I was picking up what the fish felt—and the way I was acting like them—while the other part was watching curiously (and tensely) for the arrival of this ominous newcomer. Then, like a roll on the tympani in an orchestra, a rumbling that begins below the threshold of hearing and gradually encroaches on perception until it is all we can feel, a huge presence boomed upon us, sweeping all the finicky tension before it. The small fish parted, leaving an alley two feet wide from surface to bottom, and into that alley swam three eighty-pound tarpon.

The tarpon is a grand fish. It has scales like silver dollars, eyes like a giant owl's, and a mouth that looks like a cave. The three of them that swam slowly through us now were like a trio of dinosaurs crashing a poodle show; they cast their eyes right and left with unmistakable superiority and disdain. (And if they noticed that I wasn't a two-inch fishling, they gave no sign. Perhaps my obvious awe made me just another member of the small fry to them.)

The fish and I kept our corridor respectfully open. The tarpon cruised through, waving their tails with slow, careless dignity. I (and no doubt the little fish) waited anxiously for one of them to dash suddenly into the throng and gulp down a few dozen snack bites, but it never happened. The big guys just idled along, leaving us behind holding our breath (at

The tarpon is a heavy presence.

least some of us). As they moved away, a release of tension like a collective sigh swept through all of us watchers. Then, at the last moment, as the tarpon tails began to disappear at the far end of the alley, I remembered I *wasn't* one of the small fish, and hastily paddled after the tarpon to follow and spy. I never caught up, and when I returned to the silver bay fifteen minutes later, the little fish were gone, too.

In the years since that dive, I have wondered about my experience down there in the water with the jillion little fish and the three tarpon. How did the small fish stay so close together and yet never bump into one another? How did they stay so close to me, yet never allow me to touch them? How did they feel the approach of the big hunters? How did I feel the same thing? As I look back, what stands out most clearly is that in those few minutes we all seemed to know and feel a great deal. There was simply a lot of awareness.

How did this awareness come about? How did we all perceive the things we did, and know what we knew? Take the approach of the tarpon, for example. I cannot answer for the fish, but, if pressed, I would say that at the time there just seemed to be a kind of vibration in the water: nothing you could see rippling, nothing you could hear splashing, but something subtler, something you could feel in your skin and sense in your mind, the way you do when someone in a state of high excitation enters a room full of other people. The tension passes quickly through the crowd until everyone is alert, waiting.

I am fascinated by the fact that all of my supposedly superior human qualities of alertness and intelligence did not really set me apart from the fish in whose midst I had intruded—without whose perceptions, perhaps, I might not have even been able to sense what was going on. For there was no doubt that whatever I felt they felt first; it was then communicated to me. Not sent as a specific message, but definitely communicated.

Getting communication through vibrations from a bunch of fish! Imagine! Most of us would scoff at the idea; communication, we would say, is a decidedly human art, especially when the transmission and reception are subtle. Oh, sure, lions might snarl at each other and birds might

There's not much doubt about what this gray wolf is feeling, or what it wants you to feel.

cheep, but it takes human wits to design, deliver, and receive more elaborate messages. Doesn't it?

Well, maybe not. We boast the largest brains in the animal world, relative to body size, but communication involves more than just thinking. There is a physical side to the art: messages are sent and received by the body—especially in the senses. The five senses—sight, hearing, taste, smell, and touch—represent a mysterious mix of intelligence and physique: there is an apparatus in the nervous system that perceives a sound or odor or vision, and there is the brain (also a part of the nervous system), which translates the perception into thought. As we have noted, humans have superior brains. But when it comes to the physical equipment for sending and receiving messages, we are laughably inferior to thousands of animals. So, given the fact that birds, for example, have better sight and better voices than we do, that dogs and bears have better senses of smell and hearing, and that butterflies have a better sense of taste, is it logical for us to conclude that we own the field of communication? If so, what is all this sharp animal equipment for?

Perhaps we should begin to understand that animals are equipped as they are because they need to be alert for possible communication at all times—communication not just from other members of their flock but from their environment at large. Usually, we regard the act of *sending*

We recognize expressions most easily in the faces of primates such as this black-handed spider monkey.

The defensive posture of this long-eared owl follows the rigid conventions of its species—but its message is instantly clear to any outsider as well.

a message as the definitive act of communication: we think carefully about what we are going to say or write or film, or what was behind the words or images cast toward us by someone else. But now we may do better by looking at the *receiving*, rather than just the sending. Getting a message requires intelligence and physical skill, too.

It will help if we try to see the environment the way an animal does: as a constant source of information about everything that matters in life. Where is the food? Where is the enemy? Where is my mate? These questions are constant, and the answers are always out there. Scents on the ground, sounds in the wind, a change of color among the leaves of the forest—all of these offer a tale of the moment to an alert animal. It is a tale the animal had better be ready for: any piece of information is ignored at peril. The lives of wild animals are dangerous, and efficient. Nothing is wasted, least of all information. An animal basically lives in an uninterrupted state of wariness, presuming—pretty accurately—that there is always a hostile animal nearby looking for it, or that it may never find another piece of food.

Humans don't need to be quite this careful all the time, so it is difficult for us to recognize and acknowledge the intelligence and almost athletic adroitness animals bring into play with their senses. We can more easily appreciate the wit and skill clearly involved in the many amazing ways animals *do* send messages—through song, gesture, display, dance, sign language, even chemical emission—because we are used to evaluating such behavior in ourselves. These actions are worthy of appreciation; they reveal how ingenious animals can be when they intend to say something. But the ingenuity is there in the waiting and watching and listening and sniffing, too—in the fabulous ears, tongues, noses, antennae, eyes, nervous systems. We can learn much about the world by trying to understand what sort of things animals are ready to perceive.

Of course, it is not possible for a human being to feel exactly what an animal feels when it perceives a certain sight, sound, smell, taste, or touch. We can only imagine. Scientists try to help out imagination by studying the physical mechanics of animals' sensory organs; they can describe precisely how sound waves strike a membrane in a fox's ear and set it atremble, or how the tissues lining a bear's nose absorb molecules from the air and pass electrical impulses on to the brain. And even though knowing how it happens mechanically is not nearly the same as feeling it happen directly, we can combine facts with observations and empathy to create a kind of understanding that lets us speculate pretty well.

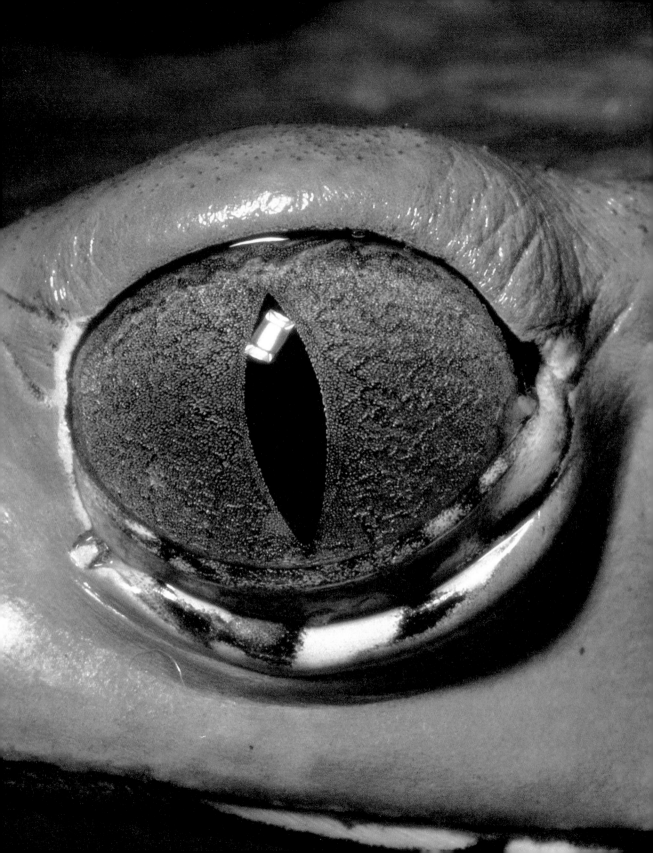

Seeing

For many of us, the first sense we think of is sight. Human beings rely so heavily on their eyes that sometimes schoolchildren learning about the senses have difficulty remembering that sight must be listed as an equal alongside smell and taste and touch and hearing. Vision seems, somehow, to be bigger than these other things; surely it is not just "a sense" but something more elemental and important—as if awareness itself begins only when we open our eyes.

By investing much of our awareness in being receptive to visual stimuli, we have unwittingly taken away some of our sensitivity from the nose, the palate, the ear, the skin. People without sight have learned that other senses can be just as quick, subtle, and reliable; indeed, some who have lost their sight say that hearing, for example, is a preferable primary sense. But most of us cannot conceive of preferring anything to sight. Consider the types of communication and entertainment that rely on a keen eye: printed words, pictures, film . . . Even popular music, which used to depend entirely on audio (radio) to spread interest in its tunes, has now become a largely visual medium. No record label releases a single for radio play without also releasing a video to MTV and VH1.

And what about talking? Well, technically, one could claim that speech is not visual communication. But haven't we made it so? Rarely do we simply speak or listen without relying on a sudden raised finger, a lifting of the eyebrows, the hint of a mocking smile, even that flicker in the eyes that reveals insincerity ("Look at me and answer me again: Did you hit your sister?"). We depend on such complementary expressions to guide us in the interpretation of spoken words.

In general, animals tend to be less hierarchical with their senses. When the environment throws out an item of communication, an animal uses the sense that will best perceive that item. A wolf waiting for the approach of a mate who has been hunting will not miss invisible signs that float down the wind to his ears and nose. If the eyes are the last to know, the wolf certainly won't wait to get their input.

Nevertheless, if animals do not share our reliance on vision, they use their eyes as avidly as they use any other needed sense, for indeed many sorts of communication can best be conveyed to the eye. Motion, shape,

The so-called four-eyed fish really has the usual two, but it can look above and below the surface of the river at the same time. The eye's lens is shaped to allow sight through the air in the upper half and sight through the water in the lower.

color do not register as clearly with any other sense, if at all. An object's shape can be perceived by touch, but unless the object is very small and can be completely wrapped by one appendage, the way we can surround an almond with one hand, the shape of the object does not come in a single impression, as it does with sight. If the thing is too large for this, the animal must cover its surface with a series of touches that are assembled in its mind, the way we might (if we were blindfolded) work our way around an automobile with our hands. Technically, one could also say that different-colored surfaces could be distinguished by touch, because different colors absorb light and heat in varying degrees. But, again, this would be a tough job. So we can say that color is a wholly visual quality, truly perceived only with the eye.

Color is the vital key to reproduction in many species. A male blue jay whose breast feathers are a bit brighter, a male painted terrapin whose red cheek stripes flash more intensely, a male mandrill whose lurid face seems closer to bursting like a ripe fruit—these individuals enjoy an advantage over the other males around them with less vibrant equipment, because females see them and then favor them. Higher visibility—despite certain obvious drawbacks when it comes to lying low—is almost always perceived as a kind of power, completely desirable or enviable to members of the same species.

But before we make too many assumptions about the role of color, we should realize that animal eyes do not necessarily perceive color the way human eyes do. We see that male cardinals are red, and we conclude that female cardinals can see the color red; but do they, really? Or do they perceive what is red to *us* as a kind of luminous tan against a deep gray background? Or perhaps as a sharp dark shadow outlined by a shimmering haze of bluish fuzz? We cannot possibly know. Zoologists have dissected a lot of eyeballs and nerve tissue and brains, psychologists have designed a lot of elegant experiments to test whether a particular species can perceive differences between certain colors, but still there is no way for us to imitate the experience of seeing in the manner indicated by such data. We can know, for example, that a rabbit's retina—the membrane in the back of the eyeball that receives images through

Both plant and animal species may make use of color in their reproductive strategies. Many plants attract animals primarily through vision, bright colors signifying nectar to drink or fruit to eat—along with a smudge of seed or pollen to disperse unknowingly. Here a bromeliad attracts an alligator lizard, and a passionflower tempts a bronzy hermit hummingbird.

light—performs much more work than a human's, organizing and processing visual information on the spot, whereas our eyes roughly capture raw material and immediately shove it off into the brain to be sorted out; but how can we understand what the rabbit sees? We can't.

Frogs have been subjected to a lot of laboratory experiments, so we have a lot of "knowledge" about their vision. They see the distance as a flat, dark screen. To be visible against it, nearby things must present certain characteristics: their color must contrast with the background; or their outlines must be sharp and rectilinear; or they must be in motion toward the frog *and* have a frontal surface that is convex. Frogs can also see if their background suddenly grows darker. They can tell the difference between green and blue; in fact, if a frog is sitting at the edge of two pieces of paper, one green and one blue, an alarming stimulus will cause the frog always to jump onto the blue sheet.

Knowing these nicely defined characteristics of frog vision, can we blink a few times and see like a frog? Alas, no; the world still looks the way it always does. We can, however, try to understand how some of these distinctions function in a frog's visual universe. What, for example, might make the background darken quickly? Well, for one thing, the approach of a large shape, such as a predatory bird. What, besides another frog, has a convex shape in front? Insects, which, when they are moving toward the frog, represent a prime food coming within reach. The preference for blue over green when alarmed? Green represents terrestrial vegetation, while blue means water: when something startles the frog, it prefers to flee into the water rather than remain exposed on land. So the frog sees just enough to flee from enemies and grasp or gulp food.

What about an animal with *fantastic* vision? Well, birds in general, and birds of prey in particular, have remarkable eyes. Human observers are often amazed by the precision with which owl, hawk, falcon, and eagle can see in difficult light or from great distance. These birds may see colors, but they are best at discerning shape and movement. A peregrine falcon circling in the wind a quarter mile up will notice the flutter of a pigeon's wings forty feet off the ground, and the falcon will drop

Eyes see what they need to see, whether in the green brightness of the rain forest or the dim shadows of a cave, in the blaze of day or the dark of a moonless night. These eyes belong to (clockwise from top left) a Jackson's chameleon, a horsefly, ghost bats, and a great horned owl.

on it like a thrown brick, approaching 220 mph yet striking it exactly in the right spot to make an efficient kill. A red-tailed hawk perched 160 feet up in a tulip poplar will spot a quick flicker in a hayfield, a small tawny motion against a tawny background, and in six seconds the world loses another mouse. An osprey flying a hundred yards above the choppy Atlantic can tell at a glance which blips of white water are caused by wind and current, and which by a small school of bluefish, one of which it will snatch from below the surface in a swooping dive.

As eyes go, these are some pretty impressive specimens—the Patrick Ewings of the ocular world. Birds of prey have *huge* eyeballs; a snowy owl's are the same size as an adult human's. To make room for the big orbs while keeping the weight to a minimum (always a consideration when nature is designing a creature for flight), some other stuff has been reduced or left out of the head structure. Birds of prey have little olfactory apparatus, for example; it seems to be more important for them to see than to smell. The large eyeball has also taken up space that might have been shared by muscles used for moving it around, so that although the eye is very big it is pretty immobile. To check out something off to the side, the bird must turn its head. Owls, with the biggest eyes and the fewest controlling muscles, can rotate their heads front to back in either direction.

Most birds eat insects, and many of them catch their prey in midair with their beaks. Insects can be pretty small; seeing one when you are flying rapidly past it, and grabbing it with the equivalent of a pair of tweezers attached to your head only a half inch from your eyes, requires not only great retinal sensitivity but great coordination between the two eyes (not to mention the beak).

For diving birds, seeing underwater just after seeing in the air requires that they manipulate the part of the eyeball called the lens—an oval piece of tissue just behind the pupil, which is where the light enters—to change the way the eye can focus. They elongate the lens, apparently, with a sort of squeeze and squint.

Fish, of course, don't need to change their vision back and forth between air and water. But they must adjust the position of the lens within the eye to see something nearby or far away through the water. Nobody

These emperor penguins don't need some kind of compound eyes to see through water as well as air: when they dive, their eyeballs shift around structurally to adjust—while the flounder's eyeballs actually migrate across its head, both ending up on one side.

knows just what fish perceive, but we can guess that they see motion pretty well: some species attract mates by waggling the tail from side to side in a kind of slo-mo swim-dance. Flashes of color or contrast get through, too, at least to the barracuda. This fierce predator, which looks as if it is about three-fifths snaggletoothed mouth, scares a lot of snorkelers in the world's warm oceans but rarely attacks humans. When it has done so, however, the reason has usually been clear: the human was wearing a piece of bright metallic jewelry or glassy diving equipment that caught sunlight and flashed it at the 'cuda, looking for the moment like a silvery fish. In the Caribbean, people thought for a long time that barracudas had very discerning vision, because they precisely attacked just the masks of divers, ripping them off and dashing away, leaving the diver to splutter and blink his way back to the boat. Then someone figured out that the glass of the masks was about the same size and shape as several species of rather slow, plump silver fish much favored by the predator, and the reason behind the mask attacks was clarified. (What a shock for the poor barracuda. One wonders if a few strikes that provide nothing but a mouthful of rubber and glass will cure it of a taste for pompano and amberjack.)

Although we can never be sure what an animal is capable of seeing, it is more important to note that other animals *do* seem to have ideas about what is and is not perceptible. Obviously, to send a message, you need to know what signals will get through; to hide, you need to know what signs won't be noticed. In general, animals dealing with sharp-eyed predators appear to have learned through the ages to assume that if they show themselves, they will be seen and probably attacked. Thus, when a vole in the forest has to leave its shelter, it hurries frantically and skitters along the sides of logs or beneath leaves, presuming that the sky is full of keen, alert hawks. Haste and stealth come naturally to the prey of sharp-eyed animals; others, whose enemies rely on fuzzier vision or another sense altogether (smell, for example), need not be so careful about visibility and display themselves more casually and confidently.

Camouflage complicates the tactics. Most kinds of protective coloring

Camouflage is a kind of passive visual deception, as shown by the common tree frog and the arctic fox.

work best when the creature holds still in plain view of the predator, instead of fleeing. This must get kind of tense. When it finds itself suddenly face-to-face with a killer, the camouflaged animal needs to decide whether its enemy is worse at seeing color (in which case the prey freezes) or at seeing motion (in which case it runs away). Some, like the cottontail rabbit and white-tailed deer, seem to possess a more sophisticated intuition about the mechanics of vision. They lift their white tails and scamper away in zigzags through the vegetation, drawing the predator's eye to the bobbing spot. The predator focuses on the whiteness ("Hey, this is easy!"). Then the rabbit sits or the deer snaps its tail down—and suddenly the white is gone. The pursuer, which had contented itself with chasing the white spot, now sees nothing.

We can conclude that centuries of experiments in either escaping or being eaten have instructed animals in the instinctive assessment of what certain other species can or cannot see. When we consider that intel-

Some animals put on a more elaborate show to foil sharp-eyed predators, such as this eastern hognose snake playing dead with grandiose melodrama.

lectually a shrew has no better idea than we do of what a shrew looks like to various species of hawk, snake, fox, bobcat, raccoon, and opossum, then it is amazing that the shrew knows how to get around the widely varied vision of such different enemies. There is no such complex problem, of course, when the shrew is dealing with other shrews. It knows what they will see: the same things it does.

This is where the most overtly intentional visual communication takes place: within the species. Perhaps the most obvious kind of showing is called display behavior, which dominates the rituals of attracting mates and establishing territory. Display is more automatic and programmed, less improvised; an animal is born with certain equipment and it simply knows when to flash it. Showing a bright topknot or long incisors doesn't convey a detailed message that arises out of a sudden need and applies just to the moment—an unexpected food source, for example, or a surprise enemy creeping through the bushes. Nevertheless, within the rigid conventions of display behavior there are often sensually subtle transmissions of information. Sometimes the visual display leads to a finer level of communication involving another sense.

Fiddler crabs live in burrows above the tide line on beaches. Most males have one huge front claw, distinctively colored, which is useful for nothing but a kind of showing off. The male crab crouches by the entry to his burrow and spends most of his time waving his balloon claw back and forth at other males, crouched by their burrows. Sometimes a female scuttles by and he waves at her—but otherwise he just hails the guys. Once in a while, one male gets tired of all the waving, and he approaches one of his fellows for a more intimate exchange, which will bring the second sense—touch—into play.

The two crabs will square off as if for a fight, brandishing their showy appendages; then, looking like knights of old at the joust, they clash. The claws clack together, interlock, pinch, and rub—but actually the engagement is much more like a mutual Braille-reading than a joust. Instead of seeking to hurt each other, the claws are feeling out the configurations of bumps, ridges, and bristles featured on each surface, until one crab concludes that the other guy's spiky knobs are finer than his own. He scuttles back to his burrow. The winner goes back to waving.

These huge claws are for hailing, not for fighting.

If a female should be watching this display, she will rush to the side of the fellow with the finer knobs; however, as she is without a huge claw herself and thus cannot assess her mate's, she has to take the evidence of the defeated male. What, really, does a great set of ridges indicate to these crabs? Ferocity as a defender? Power as a predator? Reproductive potency? In fact the big claw has functionally nothing to do with such qualities. It is an implication only; it is pure communication. We assume there is some correlation of great claws with genetic success, or else the crabs would die out. But how do the crabs know this? Each male is aware that his own claw is useless, so he has no reason to fear his competitor's. There is *some* message, perhaps merely symbolic, in the bumps and bristles, but we can never know what it reveals.

In other animals, however, we observe less ritualized messages that we *can* understand—messages that describe features of the here and now in a kind of symbolic language *we* can decode, because we see it used over and over again consistently within the animal society. Probably the biggest breakthrough in such human understanding began in 1923 when a scientist named Karl von Frisch started decoding the "dance language" of honeybees.

Honeybees live in hives, which are maintained like perfect little cities because every bee works constantly at a particular kind of task. Scientists had long known that certain members of a honeybee colony seemed to have the job of scouting the surrounding areas for sources of nectar and pollen. These bees would fly around for a while, then return to the hive and crawl over the vertical surface of the wax honeycomb in a strange way, wiggling oddly and following a kind of geometric pattern. Dr. von Frisch watched them, charted their dance patterns, and correlated these with the distance and compass direction of the flowers to which the bees subsequently flew. In the course of fifty years of study he verified that the elements of the dance—the pattern sketched by the bee on the vertical surface, as if she were a piece of chalk on a blackboard, and the degree of animation in her wiggles—communicated with incredible precision the type and location of the food she had just found. How exact were the directions? Once he learned to decipher the dances, von Frisch found they were accurate to within five to ten degrees of compass direction and 10 percent of the distance from hive to flower—very small margins of error. He broke down the components of the movements and found that everything meant something. When the dancer twitched her abdomen eighteen times, it indicated a different direction or distance than when she twitched it sixteen times; when she waggled with a certain degree of animation, it meant the nectar solution she had found was rich in sucrose, while a weaker solution was symbolized by motions that looked cooler, less excited. (The dancing bees also released chemical odors that contributed to their articulation, but the primary message came from the visible movements.)

It wasn't always food that the scouts depicted. Sometimes they would be sent to look for locations suitable for a new hive. When different scouts found different spots, they met and danced to describe the qualities of their sites to each other and a small, select group from the hive—sort

The honeybees in blurry motion are doing the waggle dance. The others will soon know just where to go to find the latest discovery of nectar or pollen.

of an architectural review board. When this "conference" reached a consensus, the hive would swarm out and occupy the chosen site.

Now, *that's* visual communication—in fact, it's practically sign language. Still, quite a few skeptics claim they are unconvinced that it is "real" communication, just as they doubt the conscious quality of a peregrine's alertness. Perhaps the reason is simply that the alertness and the symbolic language and indeed most acts of animal intelligence do nothing more than secure food, family, and territory—the three most primitive requisites for even the most dull-witted organism. So what if an osprey can neatly pluck a fish out of whitecaps seen from 150 feet? How is that any better or brighter than the obtuse frog that sees a convex

object approaching and unfurls its tongue in that general direction? The
result is the same, say these cool disbelievers: animals know only enough
to go after chow and make babies. Those are the commonest instincts
in nature. The fancy mechanics don't matter. Perhaps if the animals
showed some trivial ambitions—inventing meaningless activities to idle
away hours of leisure time, for instance—then they would command
more respect. But most animals don't have hours of leisure time. They
may play a little, but generally they spend their rest time resting.

Perhaps it all comes back to our inability to imitate animal sight. We
don't know how much of the world is out there, visible and challenging,
demanding to be considered and decided upon, because we see only
what humans can see. We also don't know how little of the world there
is, for some animals—how much they must compensate for limited vision
by using a precise kind of imagination to fill in the shadowy spots. Once
a scientist put severely distorting eyeglasses on the human subjects of
an experiment, around the clock. After a few days the gross effects of
the glasses appeared to have "worn off": the people reported they were
seeing normally through the lenses that had warped their vision just days
before. What happened? Did the lenses mutate? No; the lenses bent the
light the same as always—that is, the images that fell on the retinas were
just as twisted. What changed was the brain's handling of this twisted
information. Essentially, each brain said, "That doesn't look right at
all," and twisted things back. This is the gift of a large intelligence. We
should not rule out the possibility that animal eyes inspire their own
compensatory gifts.

Hearing

Often it is easier to be heard than it is to be seen. And it is almost always harder to be silent than it is to be hidden from view. When you move, you move against something—leaves, rocks, reeds, water, air—and the contact produces some kind of sound. Even a bird's wing, cutting through the moist, gray air of twilight over a quiet field, makes a sound that might warn a wary animal of its approach.

Termites burrowing beneath the bark of trees and earthworms wriggling under the topsoil would seem to be pretty safe from predators, because they cannot be seen. But seeing is not everything. From the outside, woodpeckers use their ears (and beaks, held still against the bark like some kind of antennae) to pick up the sound of the termites chewing the interior wood, while robins use their ears (and feet) to sense the movements of earth below. The result? A final surprise for the termites and worms that thought they were being so discreet.

Sound is a vibration. It travels in waves, which reach the ear and pass the vibration on to a bone or hair or membrane. Nerves translate this internal vibration into electrical impulses and pass it on to the brain. Animals hear differently; ten species living in the same swamp will each hear only a part of what the others do. The structure of their ears, nervous systems, and brains determine whether they can better hear sounds of high frequency (meaning that the vibration travels in shorter waves) or low (longer waves), and at which degree of loudness. Most animals can hear some medium-range frequencies; most can also hear some sounds at very low volume. Chances are that if you move a muscle, something somewhere nearby can hear you.

Because hearing is a sense capable of such broad, subtle perception, animals can rely on communicating through sound more securely than they can through sight. Animals such as fireflies and certain deep-sea fishes that flash light at one another to show identity and position are

Inside most ears is a membrane that vibrates in response to sound waves that reach it through the air. Sometimes, as in this green frog, the membrane (behind the eye) is right out in the open.

Centuries of evolution toward an aquatic life have reduced the exterior ears of the polar bear to unobtrusive nubs that can be flattened against the head for more streamlined swimming, and closed to keep the water out.

much rarer than animals that sing, croak, coo, howl, whistle, bark, and chirp for the same purpose. On a ten-minute walk at sunset almost anywhere in the Northern Hemisphere in the month of May, we can hear at least twenty species broadcasting the basic message "Here I am"—birds chortling, frogs peeping, squirrels chattering, insects rubbing their legs together. Once you begin to pay attention, the natural world is suddenly a wildly noisy place, and behind each noise is intention.

The message "Here I am" often contains a good deal of additional information. When a male bird positions himself in the top of a tree and begins to pour out his song, he is counting on his voice to communicate such qualities as strength, determination, potency, perhaps even a kind of creativity or artfulness. The form of each species' song is like a chord-and-melody structure that a bird can embellish with accents all his own—an especially sharp trill here, a deeper throatiness to the burred note there. The singer knows that his listeners (at least the ones of his own species) will pick up the implications. He knows they hear beyond the basic message and harken around the edges, for the expression that is unique to him. "Here I am" becomes "Here I am, powerful, clever, and fearsome, capable of siring brood after brood of chicks, and capable of kicking anybody out of my territory to protect my family." Or, unfortunately, some birds can do no better than to proclaim, "Here I am, at least until somebody drives me away, because I am rather weak, as you can tell from my inability to put a lot of terrifying zest into this song." Ornithologists have experimented with recorded birdsong, taping birds of the same species that sing the same song strongly or weakly, then placing tape players in certain territories and playing the recordings. The results are clear. Competing males give a wide berth to plots of land from which the strong songs emanate, but they fly right into the places defended only by a wimpy voice, ready to take over. The same may hold true for other "vocal" animals, from coyotes to crickets.

But not all vocalizations come from the simple intention to attract mates and protect turf. In addition to their songs of male proclamation, most birds—of both genders—have a spate of calls that are used to give warning or encouragement or direction in many different circumstances. Other animals show the same flexible readiness to respond to particular needs with established signals. Vervet monkeys, which live in large social groups, understand and use at least three different vocal alarms, each of which immediately inspires defensive behavior appropriate to the message. One call is used when a martial eagle is seen or heard. Martial eagles are very large birds of prey that will pluck a vervet monkey right off a tree limb; when the eagle alarm is heard, the vervets race for dense bush cover on the ground or huddle against tree trunks. Another distinct kind of cry denotes the approach of a large terrestrial predator, such as a leopard. When they hear this, the monkeys climb trees and scoot out to the ends of the thinnest branches—which will support the monkeys but not the leopard that they assume will climb after them. The third alarm is used when a large snake is seen. At this the monkeys stand up tall and peer around, moving away coolly when they see the reptile.

It is obviously essential for the monkey that spots the predator to make the right call, especially if it's "Leopard!" or "Eagle!" The strategy that removes the vervets from one killer places them exactly in the hot spot to be taken by the other. The fact that the other monkeys believe what they hear indicates that the code is clear and well established. They can assume that anyone that happens to see the danger is capable of issuing the correct warning. This is very socialized communication—taught, learned, trusted.

Is there any communication that is not social? After all, sending a message presumes that someone else is out there to receive it, even if the message is a loud song projected boldly into the sky to fall on unknown ears. An animal alone has nothing to say, right?

Well, actually, some of the most subtle and sophisticated communication in nature happens when an animal talks to no one but itself. Dolphins, whales, bats, and several kinds of birds and fish practice something called echolocation: they make a sound and listen to the way it bounces back to them from their surroundings. They send out nice, even sound waves, which hit things—fish, outcroppings of coral, insects, tree limbs, cave openings—and rebound back to the ears in broken patterns that reveal the position of the objects and, in some cases, their material makeup as well. In most cases the sounds emitted are not melodic songs or multi-pitch calls; they are remarkably consistent tones, usually clicks, squeaks, or whistles, that cover the environment with an even coating of vibration. The sameness is important, because receiving and processing the jaggedy rebounds is a lot easier if the animal knows that the initial sonic probe went out on the usual frequency.

Insectivorous (insect-eating) bats locate an object—which they hope is an airborne insect—by calculating the time it takes for the sound waves to bounce back and reach their ears. An object that is nearer will intercept the sound and send it back faster. Bats emit and receive their squeaks while flying, so their air speed and direction must be included in the fleet calculation of an object's location, especially if that object is also flying. The squeak is very high-pitched, too high for the human ear to hear, but clearly audible to bats even as an echo. Because bat ears are sensitive enough to hear both the original squeak and the echo, an interesting problem crops up: how can the bat send out a loud sound without covering the fainter echoes it is hoping to receive immediately thereafter? Bat ears are not only sensitive; they are rather athletic as well. Inside the ears of most mammals is a small bone called the stapes, which vibrates from sound taken into the ear, then transmits its vibration to a membrane nearby. However, when the bat issues a sound, a special muscle pulls the stapes away from the membrane, preventing the bone from transmitting any sound. The muscle lets the bone pop back into place an instant after the squeak is released, so it is ready to receive the echoes. This self-inflicted instant of deafness solves the problems of sonic interference nicely.

Because most bats hunt by echolocation, it was hard for zoologists to

The grotesque convolutions of the Trinidad Tamana cave bat's nose are not just for smelling: they also catch and channel sound waves.

figure out how tropical fish-hunting bats managed to find the fish they snatched out of the water on their low-flying runs above rivers and ponds. All kinds of intricate experiments were performed to figure out whether the bats actually emitted sounds that penetrated beneath the water's surface and somehow bounced back, which seemed impossible, or whether the dispersal of the bats' sound waves over the surface of the water allowed them to read some very faint disruption caused by the presence of a fish a short distance below. The answer came easily once the idea of echolocation was put aside: the bats heard the splash when a fish broke the surface of the water, and zeroed in on it.

Dolphins and whales are renowned for using a wide variety of sounds for communication in the water and above it; we can go to a music store and buy recordings of whales "singing" to each other like orchestras in the deep, and almost any marine show features belugas or dolphins squealing and yipping and chattering to a trainer and the audience. But these sounds represent only a small part of the sonic range mastered by many aquatic mammals. Dolphins, for example, effortlessly navigate their way through the water at high speed entirely by using perhaps the most sensitive echolocation system in nature. They emit sounds far higher in pitch than those used by bats, issued and received by the "melon," a soft lump of nerve-permeated tissue that protrudes between their eyes and snout. For years, dolphins have submitted readily to tests in which scientists covered their eyes with rubber cups and then challenged them with complex, shifting mazes in the water, or hunts for fish thrown in along with other objects of the same size and shape. The dolphins always seem to thrive on the challenge of a task to be mastered in sightlessness: they whiz through the mazes without grazing a wire or partition; they ignore fake fish and gulp down the real thing, sometimes with even greater speed than their customary pace when sighted.

Dolphins and whales have great brains. No doubt their high intelligence is responsible for much of their success in negotiating the environment's challenges through the use of sonic feedback: they make the most of the information their echolocation delivers. That information is apparently very sophisticated, mostly because their equipment for sending and receiving sound is so good—not just the melon but ears as well.

In dolphins, as in some owls, the ears are not symmetrically placed: one is a little higher than the other, or a little more forward. This seeming irregularity actually lets the animal assess the placement of a sound more accurately. The difference of perception between the two ears is distinct, allowing the brain to calculate more swiftly than when it has to sort out less overt differences between symmetrical ears.

Still, despite their great range of aural perception, dolphins cannot hear everything. No creature can. Everywhere in the world, around every animal, sounds are zipping through the atmosphere above and below the level of hearing. Usually, one species can hear only a part of the range of another. A cat, for example, hears the lower notes in a mouse's repertoire, including much of its normal squeaking; but mice give each

The bat-eared fox (see the ghost bats on page 17) not only gathers sounds with these things but also dispels body heat through the considerable expanse of skin.

other warnings at a much higher pitch that is inaudible to the cat, so the creeping enemy is not aware that they are wise to its approach. Humans hear a lot of noise from crickets, which produce their "Here I am" chirps by rubbing their wings together. But a scientist who invented an artificial chirping machine was perplexed when he found that crickets among whom he played it paid absolutely no attention to its near-perfect imitation of their noise. The reason: the important part of a cricket's call sails above our hearing—the part we hear is only a sort of low-toned warm-up without any particular meaning. Making a machine to imitate this stuff is about the same as an observant foreign visitor concluding that the milk cartons and aluminum cans we save and wrap up to recycle are the really precious part of our material lives, to the point that he begins giving his American friends gift packages carefully composed of trash.

Although having a limited range of hearing means an animal will miss a great deal of nature's communication, the limitation is a blessing. Being tuned in to the whole range of sounds with which the air is vibrating would be like having to listen to a loud radio receiving all of the stations on the dial at once: classical music overlaid with seventeen commercials overlaid with twelve talk shows overlaid with heavy metal overlaid with oldies overlaid with three civil defense safety tests overlaid with New Age dulcimer tunes overlaid with eleven news bulletins overlaid with play-by-play of two basketball games and one ice hockey match . . . Within this monstrous storm of sound, one would have a hard time hearing the local weather report or a favorite song coming on the oldies station. So it is with animals: their range of perception allows them to screen out things they needn't pay attention to, and react to the things they should hear. Moths, for example, have very primitive ears with a very limited range, but they can clearly hear sounds emitted on the frequency used for echolocation by most insectivorous bats—bats whose primary food may be moths. Being able to hear that the bats are closing in gives the moths a fighting chance for some defensive maneuvers. The tactics work often enough that the moths don't die out; the bats overcome the defenses enough that they get enough to eat, and thus survive. As usual, nature is not unfair in doling out the ability to hear.

Smelling and Tasting

A dog sleeping beside us suddenly wakes and stands up alertly, lifting its nose. The dog's concentration is intense as the air passes by; clearly, a story is being told on the wind, secrets are being revealed, the world is broadcasting. We, however, can smell nothing. Nothing. The dog settles down again, perhaps with a comprehending growl, but we are left to puzzle: What did the dog detect? How? Is our nose that bad? For most of us, being around animals is like being around musicians or mathematicians—we haven't been initiated into the code, and we must accept that we don't understand the conversations.

Most of us do know enough to stand in awe of the obvious excellence of an animal's sense of smell. Looking around, we see all kinds of creatures sniffing all kinds of things, and we just know they are getting far more out of it than we would. And while we may wonder enviously what it's like to glide over the Andes like a condor or power through the ocean like a dolphin, few of us could extend such empathetic curiosity when we see a fox smelling the dark remains of a dead raccoon.

In the entire world there is no more versatile nose than the elephant's trunk, which serves as everything from a hand to a hose.

As mentioned earlier, humans are very sight-oriented; we generally prefer to check things out visually first, and follow up with the other senses for details. We don't have especially strong olfactory equipment compared to many animals (tests have shown that dogs can smell things many thousand times fainter than what we can perceive), but the additional fact that we don't depend on it as keenly makes us less alert than most wild creatures to environmental scents, and less adroit at translating them into information and action. Also, since we don't go around leaving communiqués in the odor medium, we don't know where to pick up even the simplest message either, except for those we chance to pass through.

Mammals (and some insects, especially ants) do know where to pick up scent, and where to leave it. In almost every species, there is an innate instinct for how to say "Here I am"—especially (but not entirely) among males. Many possess special glands that secrete musk, oil, acid, or another fragrant substance expressly for depositing odors of identity, while others rely on more universal scented fluids: saliva and, most commonly, urine, conserved in the body and judiciously spritzed in small doses. To us—for whom it is distasteful even to consider this—urine smells like urine: once you've gotten a whiff of one wolf's pee, you've pretty much smelled them all. Not so for wolves, or for most other mammals. Their attentive, careful behavior makes it clear that aromatic signs are much more subtle than we might suppose. For example, an important part of every male wolf's day is his patrol of the boundaries of his territory— boundaries he has marked with precisely placed shots of his own urine, boundaries that are affirmed or challenged by shots from another male wolf that trotted by and noticed the territorial mark. If the second wolf's scent overlays the first in a certain way, it may mean an overt challenge to the boundary; if it is placed close by but separately, next to the first mark but not overlapping it, it may mean that wolf number two acknowledges the sovereignty of wolf number one but will keep checking. Wolf number one responds in kind, reaffirming his rule, or accepting the challenge, or suggesting some other course of action.

It's obvious that each animal's discharge smells different from everyone else's, even if all of them belong to the same species, the same pack, even the same litter. It's obvious, too, that this scent-sending is very like written correspondence. Two animals (or sometimes more; often other male wolves join in the discussion) are communicating precisely with each other in a common language. They are separated in time and place but can be confident that the messages will be picked up and understood, like notes tacked on a public bulletin board.

Sometimes the messages are chemically more complex, and more arduous to compose. Wild dogs in Africa live in packs, rather like wolves, but the society has roles for dominant females as well as dominant males. The dominant female displays her strength by marking particular blades of grass with her urine, which communicates her gender and assertiveness to other females. But the dominant male in her pack doesn't want her assertion to stand unaccompanied, because other males will smell it, too, and come running if it appears she is independent. So whenever the female embarks on a scenting spree, the male follows her, and wherever she sprays, he sprays. However, it is not enough that he leaves his mark beside or even on top of hers; presumably any male could do that, dominant or not. Such a deposit means nothing. What he needs to communicate is the fact that he and the dominant female are united—that she recognizes and accepts his bond with her. For their markings to show this, their urine must essentially be blended. This is biologically impossible, of course, but the male does the best he can, by racing after his mate and flipping himself up on his front paws so he can place his fluid at exactly the same time she is placing hers, on the same blade of grass. (If he used the usual leg-lift method, he could not get close enough.) Apparently, even the slightest delay would be detectable to the nose of a male coming by later; the simultaneity smells different, and sends a message: "We did this together, so forget about trying to come between us."

Every animal has its own unique chemical identity. The differences between it and the chemical identity of the next animal may be tiny and subtle, but they are definite. And the chemical senses, taste and smell, can appreciate those differences. What is even more wonderful is the way a chemical trace reveals not just an individual's signature of existence but, rather, the qualities of a specific biological moment: when an animal is afraid, its chemical traces will smell different from those it leaves when it is bold, or amorous, or hungry. Quite without choice, usually without knowledge, all animals register even their emotional states in odor.

If touch is the most sensitive sense, responding most quickly to the slightest stimulus, then smell is the most distinguishing. A grain of sand and a grain of salt may at first feel the same beneath a fingertip and look the same to the eye, but they do not smell the same at all—at least to a good nose. The organs of smell are connected directly to the brain by nerve cells, and the brain apparently has the ability to parse odors into an infinite number of distinct categories, some decided quickly, others only after reflection. An animal sniffing something will often linger far longer than it does when using another sense: there is a lot of information to be processed sequentially, revealing layers of meaning.

After saying that nerves carry smell straight to the brain, we cannot say a great deal more about the nitty-gritty mechanics of how smell works. It is easily the most mysterious sense, though it is also the simplest: eyes, ears, skin, and taste buds are more complicated in structure and function than noses. We do not know what gives a substance a particular odor, the way we know that a certain wavelength manifests as a particular pitch in sound. Nor do we know how that odor activates the olfactory response.

We do know, however, that marking a place with a scent is often more powerful than simply leaving a footprint of aroma. It could be claimed that odors make of every animal a great communicator, albeit without intention, to anyone else who comes along with the ability to detect chemical evidence. However, many animals are not content merely to supply information. The chemicals they release to be smelled by others contain potent, manipulative agents that trigger specific behaviors as soon as they are perceived by the brain of the sniffer. These agents, contained in scents, are called pheromones.

Pheromones can be irresistibly powerful. They can compel an animal to lay eggs, to mate, to flee, to approach, to attack, to eat, to go hungry. Once they are perceived, many such pheromones do not require or even permit a deliberate reply. The animal that gets the message simply reacts with a predetermined response. In this regard, a pheromonic communiqué is more like a command to a brainwashed subject than a note to a friend or enemy at liberty to reply. When an ant nest is attacked, the first defenders release a spray of formic acid containing a certain alarm mix, which causes all of the ants who smell it to become greatly agitated, and to open their jaws. It may not be necessary for them to deliver any actual bites, however—an attacker suddenly faced with thousands of ants with jaws at the ready may decide to remove itself.

Certain male butterflies court by coating a female with a perfumed powder that contains pheromones stimulating her urge to mate. The male uses a special pair of tiny brushes on his abdomen to pull the powder from pouches on his rear wings and then to sprinkle it over the antennae and head of the female, while the two of them hover in midair.

Ants send and receive a lot of chemical messages, many of them augmented by gesture and touch.

Once she has received a sufficient dusting, the chemicals go to work and she settles onto a plant. The male gives her another sprinkling to provoke her readiness to the final point, then mates with her. In other animals, sometimes one male's successful mating pheromone can be counteracted by another's. In several species of mouse, a female who has been impregnated by one male can be induced to abort the developing embryo by a second male, whose chemical secretion actually manipulates her internal processes so that the usual steps of pregnancy are disrupted.

It takes an animal to respond to an intoxicating smell but not always to make and use one. Many plants have come up with ways of luring insects with colors and drenching them with scents, with the reproductive goal of getting the insects to carry pollen from one bloom to another. (Brightly colored, fragrant fruits serve a similar purpose: they attract birds and mammals, which eat them and distribute the seeds that pass

Butterflies actually sample the taste of
the flower's nectar with their feet—
and then they unfurl the coiled
proboscis to drink.

through their digestive systems unimpaired, left in feces to sprout all over the place.) A few kinds of orchid complement their aromatic appeal with a visual one: they display a fake female insect that is laden with pollen. Males buzz into the flower and attempt to mate with the effigy, acquiring a lot of pollen in the effort and distributing it to another flower when they try the same thing later. Sometimes the lure of the scent is the first step in a scheme more nefarious than reproduction: several plants actually trap and digest insects, which they attract by emitting odors that imitate either a certain species' favorite food (one flower smells like carrion and traps beetles that usually feed on dead meat), or a species' female pheromones.

Deceptions and manipulations that appeal to scent are a small, specialized part of the animal world's olfactory life, however; the larger part is almost as broad and general as awareness itself. In appraising the state of the environment at any moment—changes in the weather, the proximity of food or mates or enemies, and probably a lot of things we cannot imagine—the ability to smell is an incredibly fine and flexible tool of sensibility. Odors can be detected from far away, carried well by wind or water. The nose that smells them need not be lined up neatly with the source, either, the way you often must be if you hope to hear or see something. Odors continue to appeal long after they were left, because chemical evidence usually doesn't deteriorate or change as rapidly as a sight or a sound. And, of course, odors reveal minutely specific things about the animal emitting them.

Taste is rather the poor stepchild of smell in the realm of chemical detection, because it requires proximity—indeed, touch—and the source material is usually destroyed in the act of being examined. You can smell a smear of deer musk on a leaf for three days if you like, but you cannot chew the leaf for that long and hope to taste it. Taste and smell are almost always closely related in the animal's perceptual apparatus. The two senses differ in the way their perceptions are transmitted to the brain through nerve cells: the "buds" that perceive taste do not transmit directly to the brain but are merely linked into the nerves of the skin. Sometimes, though, the relationship between the two senses is so quick and interwoven as to make them almost indistinguishable. Moles apparently use

This raccoon is reading the tales told in the wind.

The giraffe: long neck, long tongue.

their noses for perceptions that combine taste and smell (and probably a vibrational sensitivity as well—scientists can't figure out the mole's nose!). Many reptiles perceive taste and smell together, thanks to a mysterious combining organ named after the scientist who discovered its nature, a Mr. Jacobson. The snake going through the classic procedure of flicking out its tongue is smelling, collecting odors to be processed in the Jacobson's organ in the roof of its mouth; it also has a nose, with separate passages and neural connections from those of the Jacobson's organ. Scientists believe the nose receives grosser smells, while the tongue perceives with greater refinement.

Smell is tremendously important in the search of food, of course. In general, smell plays fair with both prey and predator. While a killer sniffs and follows the inevitable chemical trail of something it would like to eat, the wary animal can detect its enemy's approach with the same sense. In both cases, the telltale aroma cannot easily be hidden. You simply cannot retract your bodily chemicals. However, you can wander through places in the environment that will obscure your traces (a river, perhaps), or pass through substances that will interfere with your enemy's olfactory discernment (fragrant plants). If you're the hunter, you can approach your prey from downwind. Not all food moves, of course, and vegetarians smell seeds in the earth as avidly as foxes smell squirrels.

Perhaps the greatest example of tracking through smell is not a case of hunting. The salmon, compelled by instincts bound into its reproductive cycle, must return as an adult to the very spot at which it hatched, years before, from its egg. The journey is difficult enough physically, requiring the fish to swim many miles against currents that are often brutally strong, and even to leap up crashing waterfalls. But even more difficult must be the mental journey, the act of exactly retracing a trip made rapidly, *with* the current, when the animal was very young. Is it memory that guides the fish? No doubt, but not memory as we usually mean it. The fish does not follow visual cues ("Oh, yes! There's the old fallen tree I remember zipping past at 28 mph when I was a wee fingerling!") as we might, because the topography of land and river changes all the time as rocks roll and settle, as trees fall, lodge, and wash away,

The mole's nose and the snake's tongue perform a mysteriously complex mix of perceptions involving taste, smell, and the sensing of vibrations and heat.

as rainfall and snowmelt surge and ebb. The sounds the river makes and the physical sensations it delivers change with these variables, too. On the salmon's quest, sight and hearing and touch give no reference.

It is instead the chemical senses that guide the salmon. Incredibly, the distant birthplace, way upstream, continues to send an unbelievably clear message: "This is where you came from." Scientists measuring the electrical activity of the nerve cells in one salmon's olfactory equipment can run fifty samples of water from tributaries around its birth stream through the nose, with no effect; the salmon does not react to water even from a stream very close to its native place. But when a sample from its home water is run through its nose, the nerves snap into excitation and the whole fish is charged with alertness and mission.

Really, this is the common, ultimate symmetry in animal communication. The message "Here I am" is always answered by the environment, which pins an alert animal in a cross fire of scents and breezes and sounds and sights and thus replies immediately by saying, "Yes, here you are." We send out a proclamation of self, whether we mean to or not, and the world sends back data that confirm it: we are alive, right here, right now, among these circumstances. Communication starts and ends within; so does knowledge. What an animal knows about the environment—the storm approaching with clouds that darken and the smell of rain, the bear that is devouring a berry patch over the next hill, the batch of clams that is buried near that coral—is all just a formulation of subjectivity proposed by the senses and adjusted moment by moment. The functional elegance of animal communication, in all of the fabulous stories of flashing signs and uttering calls and spreading scents, is based on the silent simplicity of being. All of the smells and sights and sounds add up to one singularity: the wholeness of conscious life.

Leaping high against the crushing flow of a waterfall, this red salmon will not rest until it has retraced its way to the spot where it was born.

Feeling

Sometimes even a study of the sensory apparatuses cannot explain certain perceptions. Watching a wild animal for a couple of hours, we can pin down most of its reactions to a stimulus that was clearly perceived by this or that sense, but there will always be something left over, actions that show the animal felt things through some higher, stranger kind of awareness. Down there in the water with my fish, I knew this was happening: it was what I described as "vibration."

"Vibration" sounds like a goofy sort of non-scientific word, more fitting for New Age pop psychologists than keen-thinking naturalists. But actually, vibration is indeed the means of all that underwater communication, and nothing could be more scientifically legitimate as a description.

A basic truth of motion is this: when you move, the molecules of whatever substance surrounds you move, too. Sound is a good example: it is nothing but waves of secondary vibration caused by an initial stirring.

A violin string vibrates, and sets the air in motion, and the vibration in the air reaches our ears, replicating fairly well the first tremble of the string. It is the same with a bat's squeak or a coyote's howl.

If animals can take in these vibrations, perceived as "sound" only because they tickle the tiny bones of the ear, can they not take in other vibrations as well, with other parts of the body and mind? The environment—air, water, earth—is full of motion. It must be humming with vibrations! Are there mechanisms that "feel" them, the way the ears hear?

Such delicate contact! The water strider keeps itself poised to walk on water.

Indeed there are such things, and most animals have them: antennae in insects, hair or hairlike protrusions in almost everything from mammals to shellfish, incredibly sensitive tongues in snakes, trembling tissues and membranes in dolphins, cicadas, elephants. Animals probably receive more environmental communication in the form of subtle vibrations than in the other forms—things that can be seen, heard, tasted, or smelled. The vibrational perception is very much like touch and can be included here as part of the study of that sense. But we can almost regard it as a sixth sense, through which one can touch something distant.

As it happens, fish were the perfect animals to introduce me to this world of extra-touch. More than most other creatures, fish are constructed to receive vibrations along the whole surface of their bodies, as a primary means of perceiving the world. Fish have eyes, but not very keen ones; they hear, but poorly; their taste and smell are limited in range by how rapidly the concentrations of perceived chemicals are dispersed in water. (Fish smell very well, if not very good.) Sharks, rightfully famous for being able to smell blood in the water from far away, actually rely just as much on perceiving the irregular vibrations made by an injured, frightened, or weakened animal. A fish twitching in an unusual way needn't bleed to bring a shark speeding down upon it.

From head to tail along the sides of a fish's body, midway between the ventral (underside) and dorsal (top) surfaces, runs a lateral line of sense organs called neuromasts. They are essentially small, hairlike things set in very sensitive follicles that register any movement in the water around them. There are a lot of neuromasts, all of them connected to the fish's central nervous system, so the brain is informed immediately of vibrations in the water and is able to piece together a clear impression from the sequence of stimuli. Fluids are especially reliable as transmitters of vibrations. When I moved my arm in the Caribbean bay, it moved the water against the neuromasts of the fish around me, and they moved. When I stopped moving, the water grew still, and so did the fish.

An animal usually has one sense superior to the others, and instinctively issues communications that appeal to that sense. Birds, for example, don't smell particularly well, so they don't use the mammalian trick of urinating on things to mark territorial boundaries by scent. Instead, because they do hear and see rather better, they sing and flash bright feathers at each other. Fish, so sensitive to touch, often communicate by whipping their bodies back and forth to create specific kinds of vibrations. In many species, the males indicate to females that they are ready to fertilize eggs by waggling their tails from side to side in a certain way. This triggers the female to lay the eggs, which the male immediately covers with a fertilizing secretion called milt.

It seems the sea is constantly atwitter—or perhaps aquiver—with vibes. Most predators are always on the alert for the particular kind of vibration emitted by an animal in trouble somewhere. It is unlikely that wounded or sick fish move in a way designed to give an intentional distress signal, because they don't want to call attention to themselves in a weakened state. But something does change in the way a fish moves when it is hurting. Maybe the fish sucks water through its gills differently; maybe its heartbeat alters as it begins to panic. Whatever it is, the vibrations broadcast the fish's woe at the worst possible time—when it is most

The predatory touch of the starfish's tentacle sends the scallop spurting away.

vulnerable. When a fish in a school is wounded, it releases a small amount of a certain chemical into the water, warning its brethren that they can expect the arrival any minute of something predatory. The rest of the school takes the hint and pulls away, isolating the potential victim.

If we were asked to name vibrating animals outside the water, most of us would put bees high on our list (all that buzzing!). We would be right: in addition to the coded dancing we've already examined, bees *do* use vibrations to communicate. The signals they send are actually audible to us, so for years scientists assumed that bees were "speaking" when they screeched and squeaked, and "listening" when they responded to such "sounds." The trouble with this analysis was the fact that no one could locate any sort of hearing mechanism on the insects themselves. It is now clear that bees do not hear the sounds we hear them make; rather, they perceive them with the vibratory sense and touch, especially through the feet, antennae, and fine hairs in the joints around the head. The wax comb that bees build and inhabit, partially filled with fluid honey, is used as the transmitter of vibrations initiated by a shaking bee. The vibes send two primary messages, one to inspire alarm, and one to inspire calmness.

The sense of vibrational sensitivity, and its extension into touch, have the responsibility of receiving the most fundamental communication in nature, a message that is sent every instant of every day to every living thing on Earth. This message is not carried by sound, for there are moments of silence in most lives. It is not carried by light, shape, or color, for there are many times when animals do not see. It is not carried by chemical means, so it cannot be smelled or tasted. It is simply something that every living creature feels. It is gravity.

We think of gravity far less than we feel it. The pull from the earth seems to be something inside each of us, almost a personal quality; we measure our individual mass most commonly by assessing gravity's force, though we regard it as our own property: "My weight is . . ." But when we do bring gravity itself to mind, perhaps we should recognize it as a force outside ourselves, to be perceived no less alertly than birdsong. We could say, really, that gravity is the Earth's statement of locus and identity: "Here I am."

Well, perhaps not everyone reacts the same way to gravity! This species of catfish spends its life upside down.

How do we "feel" gravity? Well, we know that much of our perception of equilibrium—our balanced relation with the surface of the earth—comes from fluid-filled organs in the inner ear (a fluid will always orient itself so that its surface is aligned with the uniform yank of gravity). But no matter how much we know, it is hard to isolate the feeling, because we are never without it. In animals, too, we can study different mechanisms for perceiving gravity, but we can only speculate about what they feel like. Bees use their heads as dangling weights whose position relative to the directional pull of gravity is registered by various surrounding joints covered with sensitive hairs. Ants, too, feel gravity in their joints. Other animals have arrangements of fluid and membrane similar to ours. At least one species of shrimp has to add to its body in order to perceive the pull: after each molt, this shrimp uses its claws to pick up a few grains of sand and drop them into the groove surrounding the base of each antenna. The grains, under gravity's pull, press against sensitive cells that send the message to the brain that everything is right side up. If the pressure of the granules is removed, the cells issue alarm and confusion, and the shrimp turns this way and that until it feels the downward pressure once more. Scientists have verified this by placing a molting shrimp in an aquarium whose bottom was covered with granules of iron, which the shrimp dropped into its grooves instead of sand. The scientists then held a strong magnet above the aquarium, lifting the iron granules away from the cells—and the shrimp flipped over and began to swim upside down. When the magnet was held at the side of the aquarium, the shrimp flipped again, until the pull of the magnet drew the grains against the sensors; then it swam on its *side*!

Terrestrial animals have an easier time of it than those that spend their lives suspended in water or air. They pretty much know where to find the earth anytime: it is beneath their feet. Perhaps it takes an effort for us to recognize that every step an animal takes is an instance of critical touch—the earth is there to be perceived, and touch is the way to do it. Everything else an animal does—in the pursuit of food, the construction of nests, and so on—depends first of all on knowing literally where it stands.

There is more that the surface of the earth communicates, of course. Often, animals know about impending earthquakes even before seismic instruments alert human beings, because they feel with their feet; included in the narratives of many famous quakes are accounts of how the animals in a village or city suddenly started behaving in very weird ways, dashing around in desperate attempts to flee from the one thing they couldn't get away from: the ground.

Many animals hunt—or at least search—with their feet, like the robins mentioned earlier. Earthworms, which we would generally define as pretty low-profile types, should probably be counted among the world's great communicators, when we consider all of the involuntary messages they send upward by their slow burrowing. Lots of animals eat worms, so lots of animals are always on the alert for them. Moles in particular have a knack for feeling the faint earthy vibrations caused by the creeping worms. It is not with their feet that the poor-sighted moles feel, however; the front feet are tough and bony, with big nails, and ill equipped with nerves, and the small back feet are of no use for feeling, either. Instead, moles use remarkable sense organs in their noses to perceive a wide range of stimuli that other animals would get only through touch, taste, and smell.

Touch is a great way to gather information, as long as what you are scrutinizing can be approached without danger. A small insect on the lookout for approaching predators doesn't want to wander around until its antennae bump into a bird's open beak; but it will touch nearly everything else around it, scanning the surfaces of leaves, bark, soil, and other members of its species as it assembles a catalogue of identification. Of all the senses, touch is the subtlest: it registers smaller degrees of stimulation than smell, sight, taste, and hearing, and it does so with greater speed. But the nerves that feel also lose their keenness pretty quickly—there is a rapid loss of sensation in a touch that is prolonged (lean your elbow on your knee and see if you still feel the texture of your

To humans, antennae are a
marvelous mystery, capable of
sensitively perceiving all kinds of
things we cannot see or hear or
feel. These antennae belong to a
blister beetle (left), luna moth
(top), and flame lobster (right).

pants against the skin after ten seconds). Sometimes a communiqué of pure texture is augmented by chemical secretions that seep in through the epidermis, as when ants returning from a scouting trip feel one another with antennae and forelegs, sending signals not just with gestures but with formic acid, too.

For mammals, of course (and probably for other kinds of animals as well), touch serves purposes beyond the strictly utilitarian. From mice to monkeys, mammals express attention, affection, and nurturing care by touching each other. Some nuzzle noses, some lick, some bump heads. Apes, with their deft fingers, show their fond attentiveness by searching each other's fur for parasites. (Animals of different species groom, too: some large fish allow small ones to clean between their teeth, alligators let certain birds do the same, and large mammals of the African plains suffer the presence on their backs of birds that scour them for ticks.) Touching builds a bond between parents and offspring, between mates, between members of an animal community. Laboratory experiments have shown tremendous advantages in all kinds of factors of growth—physical health, mental alertness—in animals that were touched regularly versus similar ones that were not. (Touch can communicate the opposite of fondness, too: a wasp's sting could be considered a kind of touch, as could a slap, jab, or poke.)

An interesting thing about feeling is the fact that an animal is almost always doing it with the entire surface of the body. The beetle that feels the seams of a nut with its antennae is also feeling dead leaves with its feet, air currents with its head, and sunlight with its back. Internally, animals feel the systems, conditions, and chemicals of the body—heartbeat, blood flow, hunger, adrenaline. Obviously, there is a scheme of hierarchy in the body's registration of touch: the nervous system and brain can select which of the constant stimuli to attend to, at any given point.

In this regard, touch, of all the senses, best represents the whole experience of the animal: stuff is being perceived constantly, all over the organism, but the mind cannot attend to all of it at once with undivided attention. It is the same for us: why should our brain maintain a constant alertness to the sensation of our shirt on our shoulders, when the index finger and thumb of our right hand are attempting to seize and pluck a splinter out of the third toe of our left foot? Why should the brain verify, second after second, that the air continues to riffle into our left ear from the southeast at a speed of seven mph and a temperature of sixty-six degrees Fahrenheit? The organism, whether human or animal, comes equipped with a discerning capability. Without this, every one of us would be a quivering mess of sensation—or, at best, a constantly innocent baby. At three months, the human child does not know that the sound of a venetian blind rattling in the breeze is worthless while the sound of the telephone ringing is important, so the blinds call upon the baby's attention with equal appeal. It is only later that we learn to rate the perceptions, to emphasize at the moment of perception the input that is most critical to our moment's security. This is what the entire body must do at all times with the combined perceptions of all the senses. It seems that when the environment communicates, it can count on being perceived, but the messages must wait their turn to be filed away.

Wholeness

We are used to saying that there are five senses. We are used to speaking about them one at a time, too. If we understand that an animal's physical and mental readiness to understand the messages of the environment is indeed a kind of communicative intelligence, we nevertheless believe the messages come in neatly distinct forms, appealing to neatly distinct senses.

But when we add up all the input of the senses, do we have the whole story of an animal's moment-to-moment life? A crackle in the underbrush, a scent on the shifting breeze, a flicker of white feathers through the leaves, the feel of the dry earth underfoot, and the metallic aftertaste of food that was too little and too long ago—does this sum really give us the sense of what it is to be a hungry fox waiting to pounce on a towhee in the late afternoon of a cloudy fall day? No. Something is missing, something that flows between the smelling and the hearing and the feeling, and so on, something that translates their input into knowledge, memory, foresight, strategy, and action. Something that doesn't just receive sensory data but, rather, makes sense out of them.

Making is action; it means using parts to create a whole. The word applies very well to an animal's use of its senses: from the raw material they provide, the animal constructs a wholeness that is more than just the sum of discrete impressions. Combining all of the impressions is a quality of intelligence, awareness, feeling—all unified into an individual identity. It is this awareness that makes sense of the world.

Most scientists resist the idea that animals have any sort of integrated mental life. Experts are careful not to attribute emotions to animals, nor

The bird of paradise's courtship display is more than just a song and dance. It represents the culmination of many sensitive perceptions about everything from the phase of the moon to the full readiness of his tail feathers, as well as a certainty of how he will be perceived.

Sometimes awareness itself is a message: animals, such as this white-tailed deer, often just want to show they are paying attention.

do they acknowledge that animals carefully plan experiences for themselves, achieve results, fulfill goals. (Yet we can see examples every day of apparently decisive action in the animal world, whether it comes about by design or smart improvisation. As for feelings—dare we insist that the small finch chasing a large hawk away from its nest is not courageous, or that the dog just rebuffed by its cranky master is not sad?) Scientists like to divide experience into manageable units, which can be described individually, and then in sequence: these particular molecules enter the nasal cavity and are absorbed by these particular tissues, and these particular electrical impulses are triggered in these neural-transmitter cells . . .

But the fact that the physical nature of the senses can be accurately broken down this way should not hide the wholeness from us. It is true that the flow of intelligence is harder to pin down, and it is frustrating that the more we learn technically about the individual senses, the less we know technically about how they add up to awareness. There is a disconcerting contrast between our quantified certainty on the one hand and our vagueness on the other. We don't like uncertainty. It is hard to admit that the mental alertness and strategic motivation behind acts of perception and communication cannot be separated from the more "knowable" physical capability to receive and send signals.

But why should we be discouraged because nature adds up to more than we know? This is what keeps science going: curiosity about the unknown. It is what makes all of us head for the woods with a flutter of excitement, makes us flip over rocks in a stream bed, makes us tiptoe up to a thicket in which something is rustling. We never know what we are going to find, or find out. And every time we watch an animal making sense of the world, we get the chance to do the same.

Glossary

Antenna—Jutting out from the heads of insects are long feelers that can look like wires or sticks but are really made up of connected segments. These highly sensitive appendages—called antennae—are mainly used to touch things or to pick up vibrations in the air or water; some, however, can detect scent, too. Insects possess one pair of antennae, but crustaceans, such as the lobster, boast two pairs.

Appendage—This is a smaller body part attached to a larger body part. Arms, legs, hands, feet, fins, tails, and antennae are all appendages.

Bird—If an animal has feathers, it belongs to this class of vertebrates. Most birds fly and use this gift in all parts of their lives, but some do not; one (the kiwi) does not really even have wings. Birds live very intensely—they are amazingly quick and sensitive, and their hearts beat up to ten times faster than ours do (they are warm-blooded, with a body temperature as much as 12 degrees higher than humans). In North America, we see more of them in the spring and summer because many species fly south to spend the winter in warmer parts of the world (this is called migration).

Environment—An environment is the physical surroundings—everything from rocks and air to plants and animals—among which an animal lives.

Fish—These animals are aquatic vertebrates that swim by undulating their bodies, maneuvering with fins. They inhabit the fresh and salt water of all regions, from the polar to the tropical, in a vast range of sizes. To breathe, they extract oxygen from water through gills. Most fish are predators; most lay eggs; and most are covered by scales.

Hierarchical—A hierarchy is an organizing system in which things (or groups of things) are ranked according to importance and power, one above another.

Insect—This is the largest class of animals in the world: there are about 800,000 known species, and more are being discovered all the time. Insects are invertebrates—they have no skeletons inside. Their adult bodies are divided into three segments (head, thorax, abdomen); they all have six legs, two compound eyes, and a pair of antennae; most have one or two pairs of wings. They live in more places in the world than any other kind of creature, in larger populations. One well-known scientist said to another, "What would life be like if the insects took over the world?" The second scientist laughed and said, "My dear sir, haven't you noticed they already have?"

Instincts—Animals are born with knowledge about how to live their kind of life. The interior mechanism that supplies this knowledge and puts it into involuntary use is instinct. Instinct gives spiders a mental blueprint for their webs; it makes newly hatched chickens hunker down and peep in terror when a V-shaped shadow passes by them, though they have never seen such a shadow cast by a real hawk (for that matter, neither have they seen what a hawk likes to do to a chicken). When we watch animals, we are amazed at how self-sufficient they are. Instincts are the reason they are able to take such detailed care of themselves, with so little study or instruction. But however exact instincts may be, they do not equip animals to solve unexpected problems with analytical intelligence; instincts are rigid instructions that can only be rigidly applied.

Mammal—We are pretty familiar with the vertebrate class called mammals; humans belong here, alongside dolphins, dogs, elephants, rats, whales, and lots of other warm-blooded creatures that give birth to living young (except for the oddball platypus and echidna, which lay eggs) and feed them milk. Mammals have one set of replacement teeth, fingernails or claws or hoofs, large brains, and hair. Most mammals walk the land on four legs, though quite a few have adapted to life in the water, some merely showing vestiges of their quadrupedal structure; only one group, the bats, can truly fly, though several other species spread flaps of skin and glide.

Nervous system—All through the body, from the surface of the skin to the deepest interior organs, runs a network of fibers capable of carrying impulses to and from the brain. These fibers are called nerves. The impulses, which can be detected and measured as a kind of energy not unlike electricity, communicate everything from simple physical sensation to complicated information. Indeed, we could say the nervous system is the body's way of communicating with itself: the tip of a finger feels heat and "tells" the brain; the brain decides if the degree of heat is harmful and, if so, "tells" the finger to pull back. Essentially, it is the nervous system that allows us to perceive, to feel, to think—to be aware.

Pheromone—Many animals can release chemicals for the purpose of stimulating a specific response in another animal. Such a chemical is called a pheromone. Pheromones can alarm, attract, repel, nauseate, excite, soothe—they are very powerful, sometimes even irresistible, in causing their intended effects.

Predator—An animal that kills other animals for food is a predator.

Species—A type of animal that is different from others by reason of physical or geographical distinctions is said to be a species. It's simply a word for the units of individuality in the natural world. Sometimes the distinctions between one species and another are very slight, but generally they follow the animals' own rules of division, mainly expressed in breeding habits: creatures tend to mate within their own species.

Acknowledgments
and Photo Credits

The Knowing Nature Books are inspired by the broad spirit of inquiry and richness of detail in the NATURE television series. The books are original works, however, and their material is not derived from the NATURE programs. Thanks to those at Thirteen/WNET in New York: George Page and Fred Kaufman at NATURE, and Ruth Ann Burns at the Educational Resources Center. NATURE is presented in association with The Nature Conservancy, and is made possible with the generous support of Public Television Stations, the American Gas Association (A.G.A.), Siemens Corporation, and Canon U.S.A., Inc.

Personal thanks to the people who have helped make the book: David Wolff, Margaret Ferguson, Elaine Chubb, and David Reisman.

Cover photo is of horned puffins; photo on title page, an owl monkey; photo on page vi, school of baitfish; photo on page 10, a tree frog; photo on page 28, an African elephant; photo on page 38, a musk-ox; photo on page 52, a toothpick grasshopper; and photo on page 64, an orangutan.

10   © Jeff Lepore, National Audubon Society Collection/Photo Researchers, Inc.

12   © Zig Leszczynski/Animals Animals

14 (top)   © G. I. Bernard, Oxford Scientific Films/Animals Animals

14 (bottom)   © Michael Fogden/Animals Animals

16 (top)   © Bruce Davidson/Animals Animals

16 (bottom)   © Hans Halberstadt, National Audubon Society Collection/Photo Researchers, Inc.

17 (top)   © Oxford Scientific Films/Animals Animals

17 (bottom)   © Tom McHugh, National Audubon Society Collection/Photo Researchers, Inc.

19 (top)   © William Curtsinger, National Audubon Society Collection/Photo Researchers, Inc.

19 (bottom)   © David Hall, National Audubon Society Collection/Photo Researchers, Inc.

21 (top)   © Perry D. Slocum/Animals Animals

21 (bottom)   © Breck P. Kent/Animals Animals

22   © Jack Dermid, National Audubon Society Collection/Photo Researchers, Inc.

24   © John L. Pontier/Animals Animals

26   © Scott Camazine, National Audubon Society Collection/Photo Researchers, Inc.

28   © M. P. Kahl, National Audubon Society Collection/Photo Researchers, Inc.

30   © Zig Leszczynski/Animals Animals

31   © Stephen J. Krasemann, National Audubon Society Collection/Photo Researchers, Inc.

34   © Raymond A. Mendez/Animals Animals

36   © Arthur Gloor/Animals Animals

38   © Jeff Lepore, National Audubon Society Collection/Photo Researchers, Inc.

40   © Jim & Julie Bruton, National Audubon Society Collection/Photo Researchers, Inc.

44   © Dr. Paul A. Zahl, National Audubon Society Collection/Photo Researchers, Inc.

45 (top)   © Raymond A. Mendez/Animals Animals

45 (bottom)   © J. H. Robinson, National Audubon Society Collection/Photo Researchers, Inc.

47 (top)   © Norvia Behling/Animals Animals

47 (bottom)   © John Chellman/Animals Animals

49 (top)   © Michael Habicht/Animals Animals

49 (bottom)   © Larry Miller, National Audubon Society Collection/Photo Researchers, Inc.

51   © Dan Guravich, National Audubon Society Collection/Photo Researchers, Inc.

52   © Jeff Lepore, National Audubon Society Collection/Photo Researchers, Inc.

54   © Hermann Eisenbeiss, National Audubon Society Collection/Photo Researchers, Inc.

56   © Dr. Paul A. Zahl, National Audubon Society Collection/Photo Researchers, Inc.

58   © Miriam Austerman/Animals Animals

60   © Patti Murray/Animals Animals

61 (top)   © Breck P. Kent/Animals Animals

61 (bottom)   © E. R. Degginger/Animals Animals

64   © John Chellman/Animals Animals

66   © Michael Dick/Animals Animals

67   © Jeff Lepore, National Audubon Society Collection/Photo Researchers, Inc.

Index

Date Due

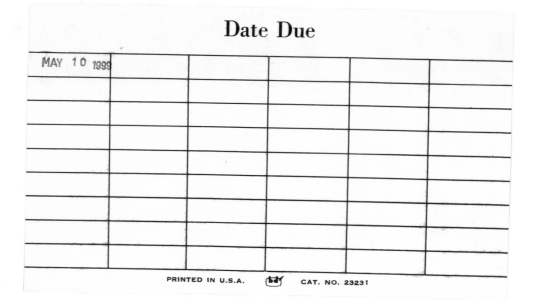

MAY 10 1999					